Read & Resp

SECTION 1

Street Child

SECTION 2

Guided reading

SECTION 3

Shared reading

SECTION 4

Plot, character and setting

SECTION 5

Talk about it

SECTION 6

Get writing

SECTION 7

Assessment

Read & Respond

FOR KS2

Author: Nikki Gamble

Development Editor: Simret Brar

Assistant Editor: Marion Archer

Series Designer: Anna Oliwa

Designer: Liz Gilbert

Designed using Adobe InDesign

Published by Scholastic Ltd,
Book End, Range Road, Witney,
Oxfordshire OX29 0YD
www.scholastic.co.uk

Printed by Bell & Bain
7 8 9   4 5 6 7 8
British Library Cataloguing-in-Publication Data
A catalogue record for this book is available from the British Library.
ISBN 978-1407-11398-2

Acknowledgements

The publishers gratefully acknowledge permission to reproduce the following copyright material: **David Higham Associates** for the use of extracts from *Street Child* by Berlie Doherty © 1993, Berlie Doherty (1993, HarperCollins Publishers) and for the use of an extract from *Street Child Playscript* (Plays Plus) by Berlie Doherty © 2008, Berlie Doherty (2008, Collins Educational). **Ragged School Museum** for the use of an extract from *Street Cries* © 1987, Ragged School Museum Trust. Every effort has been made to trace copyright holders for the works reproduced in this book, and the publishers apologise for any inadvertent omissions.

Street Child

SECTION 1

About the book

Street Child is set in the second half of the 19th century and tells the story of Jim Jarvis, a real-life character whose plight inspired Dr Barnardo to set up his children's homes.

The novel charts Jim's search for a home, starting with his family's eviction from their accommodation when his terminally sick mother is unable to pay the rent. In a journey which charts his experiences, Jim meets many characters, some of whom offer support and friendship while others seek to exploit him. Eventually Jim is rescued from a harsh life on the streets by philanthropist Dr Barnardo, and at last he finds the 'home' that he has been desperately seeking. The story is told chronologically, with a short introduction in which Jim is invited to tell his story.

The story is rich in historical detail, illuminating the lives of the street children, the workhouse inmates, the lightermen, whelk sellers, servants and circus performers. For this reason there are strong cross-curricular links with the history topic the Victorians. The book will also stimulate interest in the life of a famous Victorian, Dr Barnardo.

About the author

Berlie Doherty was born in Knotty Ash, Liverpool, in 1943. Her interest in writing was encouraged by her father, Walter Hollingsworth, who was noted among his fellow workers for his storytelling skills. As a child, Berlie was an avid reader. She particularly enjoyed character-led stories such as *Little Women*, *Heidi*, the *What Katy Did* series and Dickens' novels.

After leaving Upton Hall Convent School, Berlie studied English at the University of Durham and then Social Science at the University of Liverpool. She later trained to be an English teacher. Her teaching certificate included a creative writing course, for which she had to write a short story. This short story was later broadcast on Radio Sheffield. The radio station then commissioned her to write for a schools series, and this was the start of a writing career that was to blossom and grow.

Berlie became a full-time writer in 1983. She is a writer of great versatility and has written books for all ages, from picture books such as *Blue John* and *Jinnie Ghost* to junior novels such as *Street Child* and *Children of Winter* and teenage novels like *Daughter of the Sea* and *Deep Secret.* Berlie has also adapted several of her novels for the stage, including *Street Child*, and has written original radio plays, poetry and libretti for children's operas.

A writer of beautifully crafted prose and thoughtful characterisation, Berlie has attracted critical acclaim with her novels. She has twice won the prestigious Carnegie Medal, for teenage novels *Granny was a Buffer Girl* (1986) and *Dear Nobody* (1991).

Facts and figures

Street Child was first published by HarperCollins in 1994. It was nominated for the Carnegie Medal and shortlisted for the Sheffield Award and the Federation of Children's Book Groups Award. Its popularity saw it abridged for BBC radio in 2000 (see www.bbc.co.uk/schoolradio/english/streetchild.shtml).

Guided reading

SECTION 2

Managing the guided reading sessions

Street Child is an ideal guided reading choice for experienced Year 4 readers and older children. It is short, with a fast-moving plot and language that is rich but not inaccessible. It provides children with many opportunities for expanding their vocabulary and developing inferential reading skills.

Prior to reading the novel, introduce the children to the idea of keeping a reading log or journal. Explain that they should note their responses to the story in this log and that their jottings will be used to generate discussion. They should also write down any questions that arise while they are reading, for example, questions something that they don't understand or find strange. Ask them to keep notes of unfamiliar vocabulary so that definitions can be checked later in the dictionary and to highlight any language they find particularly appealing.

Use a range of questions and prompts. In particular, allow the children to develop personal responses. Select questions that relate the text to their experiences and probe the novel's themes. Encourage the children to ask each other questions and invite genuine discussion during which they can explore ideas.

Before reading

Write the title *Street Child* on the board. What does the title suggest? Invite the children to jot down ideas and then share them in pairs. Invite suggestions and list them on the board. Now look at the jacket cover. Ask the children whether this gives any further clues. When and where do they think the story is set?

Read the first two pages of the book. Who is telling the story? Ask the children how they imagine Barnie may have changed Jim's life.

In preparation for the guided reading session, ask the children to read Chapters 1–3 and to make notes in their journals. Identify historical vocabulary and give definitions.

Hard times (Chapters 1–3)

Invite an initial response by asking the children to tell you what they thought about while reading. Ask them to share notes from their journals, initially without comment to encourage an open response.

Ask the children to think about Jim's home. Prompt them to consider the supportive family relationships as well as the more obvious poverty-stricken conditions. What evidence can they find to support the view that this is a loving family? (In spite of her sickness, Jim's mother puts the needs of her children first; Lizzie is concerned that some pie should be saved for her mother.)

Suggest that the children consider why Emily insists that their mother is not sick and why she sighs when Jim confesses to buying the pie (Chapter 2). Do these episodes tell us anything about the differences between the two children?

What views are expressed about the workhouse? Ask the children to predict what they think will happen to Jim and his mother.

In preparation for the next session, ask the children to read Chapters 4–7. Draw attention to new vocabulary and find definitions.

The workhouse (Chapters 4–7)

Share responses from the children's reading journals. Ask the children whether they found anything unusual or surprising in these chapters. Encourage them to respond freely.

Re-read Chapter 5 from: *'I want to go home,' he said* to: *...forgotten how to smile.* Also re-read from: *Jim had no idea...* to the end of the chapter. Ask: *Why doesn't Jim regard the workhouse as 'home'? What is the difference between a house and a home?*

Ask the children to talk about any words or phrases that they particularly like. Draw attention to figurative language, such as *Her teeth were as black and twisted as the railings in the yard.* Discuss the effectiveness and appropriateness of this simile. Further examples include the collective noun *a worry of voices* and the verb choice in *The doors groaned to.*

Guided reading

SECTION 2

During independent reading, ask the children to read to the end of Chapter 10. Briefly discuss some of the jobs that people did in Victorian Britain (street sweeper, knocker-upper, whelk seller and dairywoman).

Taking flight (Chapters 8–10)

Invite the children in pairs to share responses from their reading journals. Ask: *What feelings did you experience when you read these chapters?* Encourage them to extend their responses by saying *Tell me more about that...* and to support their opinions with references to the text.

Jim meets a number of characters in these chapters. How do they respond to him? Why doesn't the street sweeper want Jim's clothes even though they are better than his own rags? Invite the children to think about why the cook takes Jim into the kitchen even though the previous cook was dismissed for harbouring his sisters. Explore this further using hot-seating. Guide the children's reflections in this activity to help them think more deeply about the characters' thoughts, feelings and motivations.

Ask the children to read to the end of Chapter 12 in independent reading. Ask: *What do you think will happen to Jim now?*

Finding Rosie (Chapters 11–12)

Ask the children if they have any questions about what they have read. Encourage them to respond to each other's questions so that a genuine discussion is initiated. Then re-read the end of Chapter 11 together and ask them what they think has happened to Emily and Lizzie. Does Jim believe Rosie's story? Ask the children to reflect on Jim's behaviour regarding school. Do they think his behaviour is justified? Invite the children to share their first impressions of Grimy Nick and to predict what will happen next.

During independent reading, ask the children to read to the end of Chapter 15. Scaffold their reading by introducing some of the historical ideas and vocabulary that they will encounter in this section (*lighter, coal, sulphur*).

Grimy Nick (Chapters 13–15)

Share notes from the children's reading journals. Develop the children's appreciation of the setting by introducing a guided visualisation strategy. Re-read the beginning of Chapter 13 aloud to the group. Suggest that they close their eyes to help them to visualise the scene. Then ask: *What do you see?* List their suggestions, without commenting. Repeat the question until you have exhausted all the suggestions. Use this technique with the other senses, for example, *What can you hear?* Read the children's ideas. Explain that when we read we build pictures in our head and that well-written text helps us to do this.

Ask the children what life with Grimy Nick must be like. In pairs, ask the children to hot-seat Jim, then gather the group to summarise ideas.

Re-read the last paragraph of Chapter 15 and ask the children to consider how the description of the setting reflects Jim's mood. Ask the children what they would do next if they were in Jim's position. Consider the strengths and weaknesses of their suggestions.

Ask the children to read to the end of Chapter 19, recording their thoughts, feelings and questions in their reading journals.

Attempting to escape (Chapters 16–19)

Invite the children to share notes from their reading journals. In pairs, ask the children to discuss the question: *Is Grimy Nick a complete villain?* Share ideas and deepen the discussion if necessary. Re-read Chapter 16 to: *Just pretend he ain't there at all.* Ask: *What do we learn about Nick and what do we learn about Jim?* Also draw attention to the episode in Chapter 17 in which Jim saves Nick's life. Ask the children why they think Nick cries. Ask them why Jim is concerned that he might have killed Nick.

In preparation for the next guided reading session, ask the children to read on to the end of Chapter 23.

In search of a home (Chapters 20–23)

Ask the children whether there is anything they find interesting or puzzling in this section. Invite them to discuss issues arising from their responses. What do they imagine Jim thinks when he first sees the circus? Ask them to highlight words or phrases to support their ideas. Draw attention to the description of the circus tent in Chapter 20: *The tent was like a huge green bird that wouldn't lie still.* Ask what visual picture this creates. Re-read from *It was then, as the horses turned with a swish…* to the end of the chapter. Ask the children what they think has happened.

Re-read Chapter 21 from *Jim crawled between the crates* to the end of the chapter. Ask: *How does Jim's behaviour here compare with his behaviour in Chapter 1?* (Jim puts Shrimps' needs before his own, whereas in the first chapter he was most concerned with satisfying his own hunger.)

In preparation for the next session, ask the children to read to the end of the book.

Home at last (Chapter 24 to the end)

Ask the children how they imagine that Jim's life will change. Ask them what they thought were the most important ideas in this book (home, belonging, friendship, family, trust and the treatment of children). Encourage them to give a free response, since there are no right answers.

In pairs, ask them to write a blurb for the book jacket. Compare what they have written with the publisher's blurb.

As a final reflection, ask the children whether they would recommend this book to a friend.

Shared reading

SECTION 3

Extract 1

- Read an enlarged copy of Extract 1, which introduces Jim and provides an insight into his family's circumstances and the concept of 'home', an underlying theme in *Street Child.* Explain to the children that character is built through action and dialogue.
- Prime three children to read the dialogue. An interactive readers' theatre approach will help to bring the extract to life.
- Read the passage expressively and elicit first responses by asking: *What came into your mind when we read this passage?* Ask the children to discuss in pairs before sharing responses. Extend first responses by encouraging them to say more, for example, *Tell me more about why you think that...*
- Build a picture by asking the children to imagine they are inside Jim's home. *What do they see/hear/smell?* Re-read the first sentence of the extract and ask: *What is the difference between a home and a house?*
- Invite the children to describe Jim in three words (excited, selfish, pleased). Ask: *What clues in the text led you to choose those words?* Annotate the text, drawing attention to the speech verb *he sang out*, dialogue *I'll have it!* and action *panting with triumph and excitement.* What do these clues tell us? Is Jim a likeable character?

Extract 2

- Read Extract 2 with the class and explain that this scene establishes the historical setting.
- After reading aloud, invite the children to sketch the picture they have in their mind's eye of the schoolroom.
- Use the sketches as a basis for children to share their first responses. Ask them whether they found anything strange or unusual about this school. How does the workhouse school differ from their experience of school? Highlight key words and phrases that describe the historical setting (*a long dim room with candles*).
- Ask the children what they think of the women's behaviour. Why do the women shout out the wrong answers and refuse to speak when Tip invites them to answer the schoolmaster's question?
- Highlight and check the children's understanding of phrases such as *mumbling to each other in low drones* and *pursed their lips.* Encourage them to use a dictionary to look up unfamiliar words as necessary. Finally, make sure the children understand the words and phrases in context.

Extract 3

- Read Extract 3 together, reading expressively to highlight the drama.
- Invite the children to share the feelings evoked by this passage. Explain that the writer has carefully built suspense so that the reader will feel tension and anticipation.
- Ask pairs of children to re-read the first three paragraphs and highlight the text by identifying the sounds (*howls, hollered, pummelled, flapping, snapped, rustling, snuffling* and *panting*). Consider the effect the words create.
- Re-read the fourth paragraph and ask the children how this contrasts with the previous paragraphs. Ask: *In the final paragraph, who is asking the questions? What effect does this have?*
- In groups, ask them to re-read the passage using sound effects to emphasise the contrast between the noisy chase and the silence that follows.

Extract 1

The Shilling Pie

At last he came to his home, in a house so full of families that he sometimes wondered how the floors and walls didn't come tumbling down with the weight and noise of them all. He ran up the stairs and burst into the room his family lived in. He was panting with triumph and excitement.

'I've got the pie! I've got the pie!' he sang out.

'Sssh!' His sister Emily was kneeling on the floor, and she turned round to him sharply. 'Ma's asleep, Jim.'

Lizzie jumped up and ran to him, pulling him over towards the fire so they could spread out the pudding cloth on the hearth. They broke off chunks of pastry and dipped them into brimming gravy.

'What about Ma?' asked Lizzie.

'She won't want it,' Emily said. 'She never eats.'

Lizzie pulled Jim's hand back as he was reaching out for another chunk. 'But the gravy might do her good,' she suggested. 'Just a little taste. Stop shovelling it down so fast, Jim. Let Ma have a bit.'

She turned round to her mother's pile of bedding and pulled back the ragged cover.

'Ma,' she whispered. 'Try a bit. It's lovely!'

She held a piece of gravy-soaked piecrust to her lips, but her mother shook her head and turned over, huddling her rug round her.

'I'll have it!' said Jim, but Lizzie put it on the corner of her mother's bed-rags.

'She might feel like it later,' she said. 'The smell might tempt her.'

'I told you,' said Emily. 'She don't want food no more. That's what she said.'

Extract 2

Tip

The schoolroom where the boys spent every morning was a long, dim room with candles set into every other desk. The little window had been painted over so they couldn't look out. There was a fireplace at one end with sheets steaming round it. Old women sometimes wandered in to see to the sheets, putting wet ones up and taking down the dry ones to be packed off back to the big houses. These were the washerwomen, and this was their workhouse job, washing the clothes of the rich. The women would sit by the fire from time to time, mumbling to each other in low drones during the lessons, sometimes cackling out remarks to the boys or shouting out the wrong answers to the deaf old schoolmaster's questions.

There were four big arches across the ceiling with letters on them, and Mr Barrack would begin every day by pointing at the arches and then by asking one of the boys to read out the words on them. 'God is good, God is holy, God is just, God is love,' the women would chant out before the boys had a chance, sometimes in the wrong order just for fun, and they would nudge each other and screech with laughter. One morning when it was Tip's turn to answer the question he turned to the women and held out his hand for them to speak. They shook their heads and pursed their lips, shaking with silent laughter, and Tip, taken by surprise, laughed out loud. Mr Barrack shook him by the back of his jacket, half lifting him off the floor.

'There's nothing to laugh at here,' he shouted.

'No sir, there ain't,' agreed Tip, and was given another shaking. The women loved this.

Extract 3

Away

Instantly Snipe was awake. His howls rang across the night. He strained to pull against the rope, in a fury to be free. Grimy Nick hollered himself into wakefulness and pummelled his fists against the hatch. Across the fields all the backyard animals sent up their clamour. Lights blazed across the water.

Jim sprinted on steadily, head down, dodging between bushes and trees. He could hear his own breathing, and the flapping of his boot soles. Brambles tore at his breeches and his jacket. An overhanging branch snapped at his cap and held it trapped, and Jim had to run back and tear it free. He loped on, his chest tight and bursting, his legs as heavy as lead weights. He had no idea where he was going.

He heard rustling in the undergrowth behind him and knew that he was being followed. The rustling became a snuffling and panting. It was a dog. Jim's leg hurt so much now that he couldn't run any further. In total weariness he flung himself down, head-first, covered his face with his hands, and waited for Snipe to spring.

He was aware that everything had gone silent again, as if the world had sunk back into sleep. At last he made himself turn his head. The dog was not Snipe at all, but a small terrier. He licked Jim's outstretched hand and ran away again through a hedge. There wasn't a sound. If Snipe still howled, he couldn't be heard from here. If Nick still hammered and swore then the noise he made was lost in the night.

'What if they're dead, bruvver?' the voice crept into his head. 'What if old Nick's suffocating down there in the hold? What if Snipe's strangled himself on that rope?' He sat up, drenched with cold sweat. 'What if you've killed them?'

Plot, character and setting

Tracking the story

Objective: To understand how writers use structure to create coherence and impact.
What you need: Copies of *Street Child*, a chapter plan and reading journals or notebooks.

What to do

- Carry out this activity during the course of reading the novel since it is intended to be ongoing. It allows children to keep a record of their responses to key events and provides a tool for reflection.
- Provide a chapter plan for the story using chapter titles. Draw attention to the way each chapter has a key moment. Ask the children to identify the key moment of each chapter and to illustrate it with a quotation from the text.
- Ask the children to annotate each key moment with reflective responses, questions, queries and connections to other books.
- Periodically reflect on what has been read so far by sharing notes.
- Highlight chapter openings and endings and discuss their effectiveness in encouraging the reader to read on and in providing satisfying outcomes to each episode.
- Encourage the children to comment on each other's ideas and extend their thinking by inviting them make challenging statements that require justification (for example, *I don't agree that Grimy Nick is a complete villain because he weeps when Jim saves his life*).

Differentiation
For older/more confident learners: Develop discussion and peer response. Model how to invite and offer feedback in order to promote thinking.
For younger/less confident learners: Children can draw the thing they found most interesting in each chapter. Demonstrate how to annotate drawings.

Jim

Objective: To identify the main characteristics of a key character and to chart a character's development.
What you need: Copies of *Street Child* and photocopiable page 15.

What to do

- Carry out this activity at the beginning of the novel and then towards the end, after the children have read Chapter 24. It requires the children to read closely in order to look at how a character develops.
- Cut out the character trait cards on photocopiable page 15.
- Re-read Chapter 1 with the children.
- Organise the children into pairs. Distribute the character trait cards and check the children's understanding of them using dictionaries as needed. Ask the class to discuss the appropriateness of each character trait and then to select three cards that most closely describe Jim.
- Encourage the children to share ideas and ask them to justify their choices. Identify the most frequently chosen words.
- Repeat the activity after reading Chapter 24 together. Have the children changed their choice of cards? Why are some words different?
- Challenge each group to suggest at least one word of their own to describe Jim and to write it on a blank card.
- Finally, ask the children to reflect on how Jim has changed during the course of the story.

Differentiation
For older/more confident learners: Ask the children to complete a blank grid, using a thesaurus to find appropriate alternatives to the words provided on the photocopiable sheet.
For younger/less confident learners: Reduce the number of character words to provide an appropriate level of challenge.

What happens next?

Objective: To develop and refine prediction skills using improvisation.
What you need: Copies of *Street Child*.

What to do

- Carry out this activity before reading on to find out what happens, so that children can explore different possible outcomes and choices.
- Select an episode from the book, for example, Chapter 6: *Jim felt as if he had frozen into his seat. His lips stuck together as if ice had formed between them.*
- Arrange the children into groups and ask each group to create a freeze-frame image of this moment. Share and comment on body language, good use of expression, eye contact and so on.
- In small groups, invite the children to improvise what they think will happen next. Provide an opportunity to refine and practise the improvisations. View one or two improvisations and have the children suggest improvements.
- Ask the children to create a freeze-frame to highlight the drama at the end of this scene.
- Invite the children to improve and rehearse their scenes, starting and finishing with the freeze frames.

Differentiation
For older/more confident learners: Ask the children to offer suggestions for improving the freeze-frames.
For younger/less confident learners: Support children by allowing them to participate in mixed-ability groups.

Escape or stay: conscience alley

Objective: To read between the lines and to find evidence for interpretation.
What you need: Copies of *Street Child*.

What to do

- Read either Chapter 7 or Chapter 17 together. In both chapters, Jim has to decide whether to escape or remain in his present situation.
- Ask the children to talk about Jim's circumstances in the selected chapter. Summarise the discussion using a table showing the positive and negative aspects of each situation. So, for example, in the workhouse (Chapter 7) Jim is not free to make his own choices, but he does have shelter and some food.
- Form a 'conscience alley'. Divide the class into two groups to form two facing lines. Leave space between for 'Jim' to walk. Explain that the two lines are Jim's conscience: the thoughts that run through his head. One line will speak thoughts persuading him to stay where he is and the other line will speak thoughts persuading him to escape.
- Invite the children to suggest examples of thoughts that each line might express.
- Choose one child to take the part of Jim and ask them to walk slowly down the alley while the two facing lines speak their thoughts. When the child gets to the end of the alley, ask them to walk back through the alley this time expressing his or her thoughts. At the end of the exercise, ask for a decision: *Would* you *try to escape or stay?*
- Finally, ask the children: *How did the conscience alley help us to appreciate Jim's dilemma?*

Differentiation
For older/more confident learners: Encourage children to think of as many reasons as possible to support their argument, and to use persuasive language.
For younger/less confident learners: Ensure these children are standing near more confident learners, and check that they are contributing.

Plot, character and setting

SECTION 4

Street cries

Objective: To collect information from a range of sources and draw conclusions about the Victorian period.
What you need: Photocopiable page 16, the song 'Who will buy?' from the film or musical score of *Oliver!*
Cross-curricular link: History.

What to do

- Re-read the beginning of Chapter 12 as far as: *...close out the faces of all the strangers...* Ask the children to imagine the scene as you read. Explain that there were many street-vending jobs in the 19th century and that distinctive calls were used to attract customers.
- Distribute photocopiable page 16. Read and then explain unfamiliar occupations, such as knife grinding. Ask children to practise reading the extract.
- Listen to the song 'Who will buy?' from the film *Oliver!* Draw attention to the way in which the vendors attract attention.
- Invite the children to choose an item that could be sold by a street vendor and to write a suitable call, for example, for ice-cold bottled water.
- Create a street scene. Orchestrate a sound collage, negotiating with the children signals for 'start', 'stop', 'louder', 'softer' and 'all together'. When you have practised, refine the piece and have the children perform it to set the scene for an improvisation based on Chapter 12.

Differentiation
For older/more confident learners: Ask the children to write a description of a busy scene in Victorian London based on this activity.
For younger/less confident learners: Ask the children to draw a busy London scene and to use it to talk about everything that Jim would have seen and heard in Victorian London.

The workhouse

Objective: To collect information from a range of sources and draw conclusions about the Victorian period.
What you need: Copies of *Street Child*, a range of reference sources, including books and a list of useful websites and photocopiable page 17.
Cross-curricular link: History.

What to do

- Read Chapter 5 together. Distribute copies of photocopiable page 17, clarifying any unfamiliar language.
- Explain that historical fiction allows the reader to experience past events by walking in the footsteps of a character, thus focusing on thoughts, feelings and motivations. Information texts are mainly concerned with conveying facts.
- Compare what we learn about the workhouse from these two sources.
- Organise the children into small groups, and ask them to use a range of reference materials, fiction and non-fiction, to research life in the workhouse. Help them to make their notes systematically by suggesting the following headings for each book: title, type of text, author and date of publication.
- In the plenary, summarise what the children have learned from each source. Prompt them to consider the merits and limitations of different kinds of materials. *What are the advantages and disadvantages of an eyewitness account?*

Differentiation
For older/more confident learners: Ask the children independently to research a different aspect of Victorian life. Encourage them to think about the concepts of objectivity and subjectivity.
For younger/less confident learners: Provide the children with extra support on research skills, for example, using structural guiders (contents, index).

Jim's journey: tableaux

Objective: To improvise using a range of drama strategies and conventions to explore themes such as hopes, fears and desires.
What you need: Copies of *Street Child*, reading journals, flipchart or board and space for dramatisation.

What to do

- This activity is suitable for mixed-ability groups after the children have read the novel.
- Ask the children to review their reading journals and identify the six most significant events in Jim's story. Negotiate with the class which events are the most important. Using the board, draw a thermometer ranging from hot (very happy) to cold (very sad) and use this to chart Jim's 'emotional temperature' for each of these events.
- Divide the class into six small groups and allocate one of the agreed events to each group. Each group constructs a freeze-frame to illustrate that moment. Jim should appear in each one.
- Introduce the idea of a dramatic monologue, in which a character speaks directly to the audience. Explain that in each freeze-frame, Jim comes to life and addresses the audience to voice his thoughts, feelings, hopes and desires at that point in the story. Once he has finished speaking, he returns to the freeze-frame. Provide time for practise and then view each frame in sequence.

Differentiation
For older/more confident learners: Challenge the children to use dramatic monologue.
For younger/less confident learners: Let the children use thought tracking, using teacher-generated questions to scaffold responses.

Memorials

Objective: To understand underlying themes, causes and point of view.
What you need: Copies of *Street Child*, a digital camera and photocopiable page 18.

What to do

- When the children have read the novel, ask them to identify its main themes (friendship, home, family, poverty, loyalty and belonging).
- Ask the children to choose one theme and to scan the book for episodes to illustrate it. For instance, the theme of friendship exemplified by Tip's willingness to take punishment for Jim.
- Explain how we put up statues to help remember a person or an event. Introduce the terms 'commemorate' and 'inscription', check the definitions in a dictionary.
- Discuss some statues that the children are familiar with. Do they know of any memorials in their area. *What do they commemorate?*
- Explain to the children that they are going to make a memorial for Jim Jarvis. First, they will plan their memorial on paper and then they will form a scene and photograph it.
- Hand out photocopiable page 18. Ask the children to complete it. Remind them that they need to recreate their memorial and to think about how it will represent key themes, for example linking arms could suggest friendship.
- Ask small groups of children to look at each other's photocopiable sheets and decide on a memorial to create. They should do this by gently positioning a volunteer or volunteers.
- Photograph and display the work. Ask: *How did this help us to reflect on the novel's themes?*

Differentiation
For older/more confident learners: Ask the children to write a short report based on one of the themes, for example, 'What is a home?'
For younger/less confident learners: Help children to create a collage based on one of the themes, for example, images that represent the idea of 'home'.

Jim

- Select three cards that you think most closely describe Jim. Use the blank cards to write further character traits.

resilient	selfish	thoughtful
kind	adventurous	caring
hardworking	lazy	brave
cowardly	cheerful	optimistic
pessimistic	lonely	loner
friendly	determined	greedy
cunning	proud	shy
naïve	knowledgeable	friendly

Street cries

- Read the following text and use it as the basis for a performance.

There were many different street tradesmen with their cries. There was the fishmonger shouting, 'fine right haddocks', sounding like, Figh, ay addicks'. The Dutch herring man, crying out, 'Dutch herrins'. So sadly. The muffin man, gaily ringing his bell on winter Sunday afternoons in his white apron, with the muffin tray balanced on his head, shouting out 'Muffins'. The man selling sprats shouting out, 'Sprats alive O'. Why 'alive O', I don't know. The mussel man crying out so mournfully, 'Mussels, five farthings a quart', as if he were singing a sad song. There was the fly paper man in the summer, with fly papers shaped like a topper hat on his head, full of flies and shouting out gaily, 'I've served the Queen, and she's alive, she's alive, fly papers'. The knife grinder calling out, 'Scissors and knives to grind, to grind'. Pushing his barrow, with the grindstone and a little can of water through the streets, until he got a knife or scissors to grind and then you would hear his grindstone whirring away as he gaily peddled to make it go round. He would sometimes make a key for you.

There was the whelk man and on Sunday there was the shrimp and winkle man shouting out, 'Fine large shrimps, tuppence a pint winkles'. The watercress and celery man, shouting out, 'Fine white celery, don't forget your watercress'. But I think the nicest and prettiest street vendors were the violet sellers, who went round the streets singing, 'Sweet violets, sweeter than all the roses, sweet violets, nice little posies'.

The workhouse

- What do the following rules tell you about the workhouse?

- The Governor and Matron shall allot the quantity of provision for each day's consumption:
  Sunday: broth, meat and potatoes, peas, soup.
  Monday: rice, milk, soup and bread and cheese, mashed potatoes.
  Tuesday: broth, pork and pease pudding or bacon broth.
  Wednesday: milk, porridge, meat and potatoes or bacon and vegetable broth.
  Friday: rice and milk, ox cheek or leg of beef with potatoes, broth.
  Saturday: milk porridge, a clearance of what has been cooked made with bread and cheese, rice milk.
- The Governor shall say Grace before and after meals. Every person in the house, not necessarily engaged elsewhere, shall be required to attend.
- All the Poor in the house shall go to bed by eight o'clock in the summer months and seven o'clock in the winter months, and all candles shall be put out by that time.
- The Matron shall take care that Girls of a proper age are employed and instructed in cookery, housewifery, washing, scouring, milking and other such work as may best qualify them for service.
- All Children shall have their hands and face washed, and their hair combed every morning by the hour appointed for beginning to work.
- The Poor shall be called up by Ring of Bell and set to work as their abilities will permit, from six o'clock in the morning to six in the evening.
- Not any of the Poor shall be allowed to go out without permission of the Governor, who shall limit the time of their return.
- The Children shall be regularly sent to School or educated.
- If any Poor are found defacing these rules they will be fed on bread and water for two days.

Memorials

- A memorial is erected to help us to commemorate (remember) a person or an event. Memorials often take the form of statues. Plan your statue for Jim Jarvis' life.

Sketch an idea for your statue that you could photograph here.

What will you call this memorial?

____

What themes do you want it to represent?

____

Why do you think Jim Jarvis should be commemorated for this?

____

____

____

Write an inscription for this memorial.

____

____

____

Why have you designed the statue like this?

____

____

Street children

Objective: To improvise using a range of drama strategies and conventions, including teacher in role and narration, to explore themes such as hopes, fears and desires.
What you need: Photocopiable page 22 and a large space (preferably a hall).

What to do

- Look at the images on photocopiable page 22. Ask the children focusing questions (such as: *Who can you see in this picture? What are they wearing? What are they doing?*)
- Ask the children to imagine they are one of the children in the picture. Use narration to set the scene. For example: *It's a cold winter's night. London's street children have no shelter; some sleep in boxes, others find space on the rooftops, safe from the policemen patrolling the streets below. Nobody seems to care, but one man is shocked at what he discovers…*
- Adopt the role of Dr Barnardo and in role, round up the children and invite them to shelter in your home.
- When the children are assembled, offer them hot soup and question them about their lives. (*When did you last eat? Do you work? Where is your family?*) Encourage each child to participate.
- Give a sheet of paper to each child. Invite them to draw a picture of their dream for the future.
- Form a circle, ask the children to take it in turns to place their drawing in the centre and say a few words about their dream.

Differentiation
For older/more confident learners: Extend the work by asking children to create a short poem based on their picture.
For younger/less confident learners: Discuss the children's ideas about the picture before they start their drawings.

Talking about character

Objective: To identify features, specifically dialogue, that writers use to provoke a reaction from the reader.
What you need: Copies of *Street Child* and photocopiable page 23.

What to do

- Organise the children into small groups and distribute photocopiable page 23, preferably enlarged. Explain that these are selected quotations that give the reader insight into the characters of *Street Child.*
- Allow five minutes for groups to talk about the quotations. What does each quotation reveal about the character?
- Encourage the children to scan the text for further evidence to support their ideas.
- Ask one person in each group to note down key ideas from the discussion.
- In the plenary session, review what the reader learns about the characters from what they say. *What do the words convey about the characters' feelings?*
- Challenge the children to think about how the quotations affect their feelings and/or responses towards the characters.

Differentiation
For older/more confident learners: Extend the work by asking children to create a short poem based on their picture.
For younger/less confident learners: Discuss the children's ideas about the future before they start their drawings.

Talk about it

SECTION 5

In the news

Objective: To analyse and evaluate how speakers present points effectively through use of language and gesture.
What you need: Digital audio recorder or video recorder.

What to do

- Set up a scenario. Explain to the children that a television company is making a documentary about Jim Jarvis' life before he was rescued by Dr Barnardo and that it wants to include interviews with eyewitnesses.
- Select one of the characters that Jim meets. Together, devise some open-ended questions ask that character. Make reference to the novel to help to frame questions that will generate interesting answers. Ask for a volunteer to be interviewed in the role of the chosen character.
- Organise the children into pairs. Ask the children to select another character from the story. One child will take the role of interviewer while the other will be the character. Conduct the interviews and then record them, using either a digital audio recorder or a video recorder.
- Review the interviews and ask the children to self-evaluate. How effectively did they communicate?

Differentiation
For older/more confident learners: Challenge the children to produce a written interview incorporating quotations from interviewees.
For younger/less confident learners: Ask the children to produce a question-and-answer style interview.

Home sweet home

Objective: To respond appropriately to others in the light of different viewpoints.
What you need: Photocopiable page 24.

What to do

- Briefly discuss 'home' as a theme in *Street Child*. The story is about Jim's journey to find a new home after his mother dies. Consider each of the different places where he stays. Can any of these be called a home? Ask for reasons why or why not.
- Find and discuss references to home in *Street Child*, for example:
  - Chapter 2: *'I'll find us a home,' her mother said. 'Don't worry.'*
  - Chapter 5: *He would find a place that was safe. And he would call it home.*
  - Chapter 13, from: *Jim didn't mind in his dream…* to: *…called the Lily.*
  - Chapter 15: *This was his home. He had to accept it.*
  - Chapter 22: *'You're going home!' he whispered.*
  - Chapter 27: *'This ain't home,' he said to himself.*
  - 'The End of the Story': *'I'm Jim Jarvis, I am. And this is my home.'*
- Organise the class into pairs for a 'speed discussion'. Distribute one statement from photocopiable page 24 to each pair. Allow one minute for discussion and then each pair passes their statement to the next pair. Repeat this one more time.
- In a plenary discussion, ask the children what new thoughts about home they have discovered from their discussions.

Differentiation
For older/more confident learners: Select the more abstract quotations.
For younger/less confident learners: Select the most accessible quotations for children needing more support.

Talk about it

SECTION 5

Readers' theatre: the Ragged School

Objective: To animate a text through performance, contributing to decisions about ways to perform a text.
What you need: Copies of *Street Child* and pens in different colours for each group and yourself.

What to do

- Tell the children they are going to create a performance based on Chapter 25.
- Revise the conventions of a play and then read Chapter 25 to the class. Discuss (or use an acetate over the text with different coloured pens) Jim's words, the coffee woman's words and parts of the text that might form the basis of stage directions (for example, *he panted*).
- Make suggestions for adding sound effects, but do this sparingly.
- Hand out copies of the book to groups and ask the children to discuss the different parts and any stage directions.
- Ask the children to think about roles within the group. (Who will play the characters? Do they need a director?) Then encourage them to practise their scene together and revise it as necessary.
- Finally ask: *How did performing the text help us to better understand this chapter?*

Differentiation
For older/more confident learners: Give longer parts to the children with more reading experience.
For younger/less confident learners: Give less experienced children the shorter parts.

Bearing witness

Objective: To use drama techniques to explore a character's thoughts and feelings as a basis for first-person writing.
What you need: Copies of *Street Child*.

What to do

- Read Chapter 4, from the beginning to *the porter clanged the gates shut*.
- Discuss the viewpoints of the different characters by exploring their behaviour. (*Why do some of the children laugh and run away? Why do some people move away when the police arrive?*)
- In groups, construct a freeze-frame of the scene.
- Animate the scene with a short piece of improvised dialogue and end the scene with a second freeze-frame.
- Share and evaluate the scenes.
- Use 'thought tracking' to discover what each character is feeling and thinking. Touch the characters on the shoulder in turn and ask questions to elicit a range of responses. (*What do you think will happen to Jim now? Did you take Jim's horse? Why did you do that? What do you imagine Jim is feeling at this moment? Do you have children? Are your children warm and safe at home?*)

Differentiation
For older/more confident learners: Ask searching questions that encourage reflection on the gap that can exist between what is said and what is thought.
For younger/less confident learners: This drama activity will give the children the opportunity to inhabit a role before writing.

Street children

- Look closely at the photographs below. Describe what they are about.

Talking about character

- What do these quotations tell you about the character?

Quotation	What the quotation tells us
Ma: 'Yes. You're always good,' she said. 'That's one thing I did right, anyway.' *Chapter 3*	
Tip: 'Tell Barrack Tip did it, if he blames you for anything. Tip'll get hit anyway, so you might as well.' *Chapter 6*	
Tip: 'I daresn't. I daresn't,' Tip whispered back. 'Don't forget me, Jim.' *Chapter 8*	
Rosie: 'Like to sail away, would you Jim? I know I would. Far away to anywhere. Anywhere would be better than this.' *Chapter 11*	
Rosie: '…I'll tell you what happened to Emily and Lizzie. Close your eyes and I'll tell you what happened.' *Chapter 11*	
Shrimps: 'Three for the price of two! You don't want three, sir? Well, two for the price of three then, can't say fairer than that, can I?' *Chapter 12*	
Josh: 'Nothing gets much better. 'Not till you're dead.' *Chapter 15*	
Nick: 'You done all right,' he told him, and taking a handful of scraps of meat out of his pocket he threw them at him, laughing at Jim's surprised face. *Chapter 16*	

Home sweet home

- Explain the meaning of these statements.

A good home must be made, not bought.
Home is not a place, it is people.
Home is where the heart is.
Home is not where you live but where they understand you.
Home is a place you grow up wanting to leave, and grow old wanting to get back to.
Home is a shelter from storms – all sorts of storms.
Home is being surrounded by your personal possessions.
A home is somewhere safe.
The place where you live is not necessarily your home.
A home is a place where you can be private.
You can be yourself at home.
The best thing about going away is coming home again.
Some people do not have a home.

Dr Barnardo

Objective: To infer characters' feelings in fiction and use this as a basis for writing.
What you need: Copies of *Street Child.*

What to do

- Read Chapter 27, 'The End of the Story' and the 'Author's Note' to the children.
- Discuss the 'Author's Note'. Do the children know about Dr Barnardo? What do they think of the story of Jim Jarvis' life? Are they aware that it was based on a true story?
- Discuss Dr Barnardo and the other characters further. Do the children think that Dr Barnardo would have been known as Dr Barnie, or do they think the author invented this? How do they think Dr Barnardo would have felt when he realised Jim had no home to go to?
- Ask the children to work in pairs or small groups and re-read Chapter 27 and 'The End of the Story'. Tell them to imagine they are Dr Barnardo and ask them to discuss what he might be thinking and feeling and to make notes.
- Share some of the groups' ideas. Then ask the children to write about the episode as though they were Dr Barnardo.
- As a plenary, ask volunteers to share their episodes with the class.

Differentiation
For older/more confident learners: Ask the children to write their story as a diary entry, reflecting on what was seen and how it made Dr Barnardo feel.
For younger/less confident learners: Encourage the children to write in a similar style to the book, in the present tense.

Life in the workhouse

Objective: To use different sources, such as photographs, to write non-narrative text.
What you need: Copies of *Street Child,* photocopiable page 28.

What to do

- Read Chapters 4 and 5 of *Street Child.*
- Tell the children you are going to ask them questions about a photograph. You want them to jot down their initial ideas quickly, without worrying about right or wrong answers.
- Display photocopiable page 28 and ask the class questions about things that they can observe in the photograph.
- Then move to things which the children can infer from the image, for example, about thoughts and feelings. *What do you find most interesting in this picture? How would you describe the building in three words? Why do you think the girls are in the workhouse? What are their dreams for the future?*
- After the initial discussion, give each child a photocopiable sheet. Ask them to explore the image and to annotate it with all they can glean from the image.
- Ask the children to use their notes to develop a piece of writing about life in the workhouse. Offer the children a menu of forms (such as, writing a poem, description, story, diary or letter), enabling them to exercise choice and to build on prior learning.

Differentiation
For older/more confident learners: Offering the children choices about the form of writing will suit the most confident writers in the class and is especially important for gifted and talented learners.
For younger/less confident learners: Support these children in inferring information or encourage them to stick to literal meanings. Ask the children to write Jim's account of life in the workhouse.

Get writing

SECTION 6

From book to stage

Objective: To use varied structures to shape and organise text. Specifically, to shape, structure and write a short scene in playscript format.
What you need: Copies of *Street Child*, music and photocopiable page 29 'From book to stage'.

What to do

- Compare the playscript on photocopiable page 29 with the prose version at the end of Chapter 16, noting the similarities and differences.
- Revise the conventions of a playscript (characters, setting and directions). Remind the children that a dramatic scene usually involves just one incident, problem or issue; has dialogue and stage directions; contains some description in the dialogue as well as in the directions; and has a strong ending.
- In small groups, ask the children to adapt a scene from the book into a dramatisation, using the narrative device of a conversation between Jim and Dr Barnardo.
- Ask the children to write their playscript following the correct conventions.
- As a plenary, compare the children's playscripts with the original scene from the book. Some groups could perform their scene for the class.

Differentiation
For older/more confident learners: Challenge the children to devise alternative techniques for narrating the story.
For younger/less confident learners: Ask the children to improvise the scenes before writing and to use the improvised dialogue in their scripts.

Children's campaign

Objective: To identify criteria for evaluating a situation, presenting findings fairly and adding persuasive emphasis to key points.
What you need: Resources about child labour in the 19th century and examples of public awareness campaigns (UNICEF, Oxfam) as appropriate to the age group.
Cross-curricular link: History.

What to do

- Explain to the children that they are going to create a public awareness advertisement about the street children of Victorian Britain.
- Begin by exploring current public awareness advertisements. Ask the children, in groups, to review one and make a list of its salient features.
- Gather the class together and share ideas about what the campaign hopes to achieve. Then look at the slogan, the image and any information that it provides. Highlight the factual information and annotate persuasive techniques. Consider the effect of subtle persuasion and the negative impact of excessive persuasion.
- Ask the children to think about their advertisement for street children. Encourage them to carry out research into child labour during the 19th century, before producing their advertisement.
- After writing, review the work with the class and encourage peer evaluation of the campaign' impact and key features.

Differentiation
For older/more confident learners: Encourage children to analyse how the posters they look at achieve their effect, for example, through design, image choice and language.
For younger/less confident learners: Construct a writing frame to aid planning and use supported composition in the initial writing stage. Paired work can also be used.

Get writing

SECTION 6

Jim Jarvis: biographical writing

Objective: To organise ideas into a coherent sequence of paragraphs.
What you need: Copies of *Street Child*, resources about the workhouse and the Ragged School and examples of biographical writing on eminent Victorians (such as naturalist Charles Darwin and author Charles Dickens), photocopiable page 30.

What to do

- Discuss the purpose of biographical writing (to bring out the human element in history).
- Think about the characteristics of a biography (a biography may be structured around a theme or organised chronologically).
- Read aloud some examples of well-written biographies, ideally about eminent Victorians, so that the children can hear how the writer's voice engages the reader.
- Consider the differences between a historical novel and a biography. (A novel contains fictional characters and invented dialogue. A biography might incorporate primary source material, letters, diaries and witness accounts.)
- Identify the key events in Jim Jarvis' life (see 'Author's Note'). Ask the children to use photocopiable page 30 to plan their biography and to decide how it will be organised, with a key event in each paragraph.
- Ask the children to use their notes to write a biography of Jim Jarvis. Encourage them to use reference sources to provide additional information.

Differentiation
For older/more confident learners: Use guided writing to consider whether a biography has to be entirely objective or whether techniques to make the subject more engaging can also be used.
For younger/less confident learners: Use storyboarding to help structure the writing and to produce a picture-book biography with reduced text.

Tell tale

Objective: To experiment with different styles to write a story based on themes from a known story.
What you need: Copies of *Street Child*, to have completed 'Memorials' on page 14.

What to do

- Review the list of themes and the photographs produced in the activity 'Memorials' on page 14.
- Select one theme, such as 'loyalty'. Discuss how this theme is shown in *Street Child* and ask the children for examples.
- Discuss other stories with the same theme. Explain that knowledge of common themes can help us to write our own stories.
- Invite suggestions for a story with the theme of loyalty in a contemporary setting.
- Ask the children to choose a theme from *Street Child* and to write a story based on this. Once they have a theme, they should identify the setting and characters for their story. Remind them that a story has to have a problem.
- Give time for the children to write their story.
- After writing, share stories using the 'author's chair' technique. A volunteer sits in a special chair to read their story and is encouraged to say more about their writing choices (for example, aspects they are pleased with or difficulties they had). Other children should offer feedback, as invited to do so by the 'author'.

Differentiation
For older/more confident learners: Ask the children to select another of the themes from the novel and transfer what they have learned to their independent writing.
For younger/less confident learners: Ask the children to work on the theme that has been discussed and modelled.

Life in the workhouse

- Look at the photograph below. Annotate it with things you can see. Then think about the things you cannot see – such as what the girls are thinking.

From book to stage

- Use this playscript extract as the basis for adapting a scene from the novel.

Scene eight

Barnardo's study. Barnardo is sitting at his desk. Jim by the fire, as in Act One, Scene One.

Barnardo: I can hardly believe that anyone could be so cruel to a child, Jim. Did you not try to run away?

Jim: I did once. We moored up to a bank in the river one night because the water was choppy and Grimy Nick was feeling sick. And when he was asleep I said to myself, 'You've got to do it Jim'. I nipped over the side of the boat as quick as a rat.

Barnardo: Good for you. And what happened?

Jim: Snipe heard me, didn't he? He came howling and barking after me and nearly tore me leg off, and Grimy Nick woke up and came after me.

Music/sounds of howling and barking.

Grimy Nick: *(lit, standing front of stage with rope in his hands)* Try to run away, would you? Leave me stranded with no one to help me? Is that what I get for all my kindness? Well, it won't happen again, see? One end of this rope is going round the mast, and the other end is going round your neck. You're lucky Snipe didn't rip you to bits. Grimy Nick saved your life. Remember that. *(Nick's light goes off)*

Berlie Doherty

Jim Jarvis: biographical writing

- Use this frame to help you write notes for a biography about Jim Jarvis.

Does he have a family? Who are they, what has happened to them?
What were the main events in his life?
Who were his friends?
What happened to him in the end?
Any other important information about his life.

Assessment

SECTION 7

Assessment advice

The activities in this *Read & Respond* title provide opportunities for ongoing assessment of speaking and listening, reading and writing. In the guided reading sessions, the children are assessed on their ability to predict, infer and deduce, to read between and beyond the lines, to sustain engagement with a long text and to express their opinions, supporting them with evidence from the text.

Various activities allow you to assess engagement with the text through drama. An understanding of the novel's main themes is elicited through discussion, specifically on the concept of 'home'. Reflection on learning is encouraged throughout the activities, with final reflections prompted by questions.

The final assessment task involves the planning and production of a book trailer. In order to complete this task successfully, the children need to know not only the plot but also to have understood and responded to the book's major themes and characters.

The task requires both analysis and synthesis techniques, because the children need to use what they have learned from reading the book to create a new text.

Book trailer

Assessment focus: To understand the significance of events, themes and characters in a story.
What you need: Examples of book trailers (a useful website is: www.rhgdigital2.co.uk/minisites/bookvideoawards), photocopiable page 32 and a digital camera.

What to do

- Explain to the children that they are going to make a book trailer for *Street Child.*
- View an example of a book trailer several times. After the first viewing, ask the children to give their initial response. (Ask: *Did it make you want to read the book?*)
- View the trailer a second time. Organise the children into pairs, and ask them to discuss and list the characteristic features.
- Encourage the children to pool ideas about the purpose of a trailer (it whets the appetite; does not tell the story; captures the essence of the book; does not present the story chronologically; has a voice-over; uses some text; interprets the story with an appropriate visual style; is filmed using different camera shots and angles).
- Introduce some basic media knowledge for different camera shots and angles (close-up, mid-shot, long shot, pan, bird's eye view, high-angle shot, low-angle shot, reverse shot). Show examples of these shots in different film trailers and let the children practise with a digital camera, so that they can see how the effects are created.
- Distribute photocopiable page 32. Ask the children to use it to plan their trailer for *Street Child.* Explain that planning should indicate what is in shot and the angle used, and identify words spoken, sound effects and appropriate music.
- Invite peer assessment to encourage the children to reflect on the impact of the trailer. Does it invite a potential reader to pick up the book? Does it avoid simply retelling the story? Does it demonstrate an understanding of character and theme?
- Although planning the trailer is sufficient for the purposes of assessment, some children will enjoy making and filming their trailer using drawn or modelled animation, or live action.

Book trailer

- Use the template below to plan your book trailer for *Street Child*.

By: ______________________________

Description of shot number:	**Description of shot number:**
____________	____________
Dialogue: ____________	Dialogue: ____________
____________	____________
____________	____________
Music: ____________	Music: ____________
____________	____________
Sound effects: ____________	Sound effects: ____________
____________	____________
Camera angle: ____________	Camera angle: ____________
____________	____________
Description of shot number:	**Description of shot number:**
____________	____________
Dialogue: ____________	Dialogue: ____________
____________	____________
____________	____________
Music: ____________	Music: ____________
____________	____________
Sound effects: ____________	Sound effects: ____________
____________	____________
Camera angle: ____________	Camera angle: ____________
____________	____________